Great God, Here I Am

Today's Christian Talks with God

LESLIE F. BRANDT

Publishing House
St. Louis   London

Concordia Publishing House, St. Louis, Missouri
Concordia Publishing House Ltd., London, E. C. 1
© 1969 Concordia Publishing House
Library of Congress Catalog Card No. 69-13112

MANUFACTURED IN THE UNITED STATES OF AMERICA

Great
God,
Here
I
Am

Contents

Preface

Great God, here I am,
  tired of the hard road, the dusty valley,
  the smog and the noise of city streets.
My hands are dirty, my feet are sore;
  my heart is heavy with the concerns of others.

I'm fed up, O God.
I can no longer stand the scorn of the indifferent,
  the snickers of those who take advantage of me,
  the despair of failure in my dealings with men.

I want something for myself, O Lord.
I want to walk on water,
  to give sight to the blind, to heal the sick,
  or supernaturally produce bread for the hungry;
  to receive a few accolades of appreciation,
  to get a medal or a certificate of merit,
  or even a commendatory slap on the back.

Give me some measure of success, O God,
  some sense of importance,
  some mountain on which to be transfigured,
  some out-of-this-world experience to give wings
  to my flagging spirit.

Is it true, O God, that I must be another Christ,
  destined to find a cross at the end of my journey?
  with the hatred or indifference of unappreciative men
  the nails that pin me there?

I know the answer, O Lord.
It is loud and clear.
It is this to which You have called me.
It is for this that I have been redeemed and commissioned.
It is because of this hard road along which You lead me
  that You grant me strength to endure,
  joy in the midst of suffering,
  and the assurance of ultimate victory.

Great God, here I am.
May the crucible of this life purge me of my lust
   for self-esteem
   and render me effective
   as Your servant.

I Am
Important

"See what love the Father has given us, that we should be called children of God; and so we are." (1 John 3:1)

I am important!
This may appear to be ~~presumptuous to~~ some; *[taken for granted by]*
   others couldn't care less.
There are people who have found their ~~niche~~ in life *[place]*
   and are ~~assured~~ that they fill it better than anybody else. *[certain]*
It doesn't occur to them to question their significance.

The fact is, I seldom feel important.
I often feel like low man on the totem pole.
I can make a living
   and even feel helpful now and then.
But I am never more than second or third best.
I take refuge under the cloak of humility and Christ's promise
   that the meek shall inherit the earth.

It probably began back in childhood
   when some childish accomplishment
   was all but ignored by my parents and peers
   or when ~~some other sibling~~ received more attention than I did. *[a brother or sister]*
Or it may be that an ugly failure or shameful deed continues to
   rattle its bones in some dark closet
   and takes the wind out of my sails
   and leaves me deflated, defeated, and despairing.
I guess I have never been able to accept it or to overcome it.
I continue to crawl rather than stand upright,
   or to hide ~~under~~ some ridiculous ~~façade~~ *[behind] [wall]*
   of assumed self-importance
   designed to ~~camouflage~~ my real feelings and inferiorities. *[hide]*

I am important!
It's an eternal truth declared and constantly ~~reiterated~~ by *[repeated in]*

God's Word that no ugliness or failure, sin or defeat
can obliterate or nullify.
No matter who I am.
Whatever may be my past upbringing or present circumstances,
my weaknesses or distortions,
I am important!

"Thou hast made him little less than God,"
gasped David as he contemplated man
amidst the wonders of creation.
I know that I am God's child.
But this knowledge is often threatened by the frustrations
of my own complex nature
or the incomprehensible agonies of a suffering world.
There are times when I lose sight of a loving God
as manifested in the incarnate Christ.
The clutter of materialism,
the scream of progress,
the pace of secularization,
the hum of man-displacing computers,
the fear of nuclear destruction —
all this and more threatens to rob me of the significance
and validity I ought to feel as a child of the living God.

But the essential facts haven't changed,
only the scenery, the passing panorama.
And according to these facts, I am important!
I am important because He redeemed me.
Even when I fall away from His purposes
to selfishly follow my own,
He jealously and lovingly reaches out to draw me back
that I may be restored to Him.

I am important because His Spirit dwells within me.
He made me His temple to indwell,
His child to father,
His disciple through whom to serve,
His own to love forever.
Truly, I am important!

+ + +

O God, now I know who I am.
You gave me my identity
   in that moment my parents brought me to the font.
You touched me with Your cleansing power
   and filled my heart with Your Spirit.

I am Your child,
   fallible and often very foolish.
When I stumble in my childish attempts to follow You,
   You pick me up and dry my tears and heal my wounds
   and draw me into Your loving embrace.
It is almost as if You, too, had been a child
   and knew the dangers and hazards of the dark journey
   and felt the pain of life's conflicts and battles.

I am Your servant.
I am to serve You in serving my brothers about me.
I do not know my future course,
   but I know where I am now.
Through the pressure of circumstances
   or the persuasion of Your loving control,
   I am here to serve my fellowman,
   to retain and further comprehend my identity
   in losing my life on behalf of others.

I am Your priest,
   redeemed by Your love, sanctified through Your righteousness,
   ordained by Your calling, empowered with Your grace.
I am destined to represent Your purposes,
   to demonstrate Your love,
   to communicate Your healing touch
   to the fractured, sin-bound creatures in my path.

I thank You, O God,
   for making me valid and significant,

for putting meaning and purpose into my life,
for snatching me out of the pit of self-centeredness
and restoring my identity as a member of Your eternal family.

In Touch
With God

"Someone touched Me; for I perceive that power has gone forth from Me." (Luke 8:46)

Men, for the most part, are living in a vacuum.
Life demands more from them than their resources can supply.
Like exhausted reservoirs in a drought, they run dry.
Shattered nerves, tangled lives, broken homes are the order
   of the day.
The panic and tension of day-by-day living,
   the personal anxieties and disasters that haunt and hurt—
   is it any wonder that emotional ailments multiply?
   that character breaks down?
   that hope fails and faith goes to pieces?

But I do know men facing up to comparable pressures and
   tensions
   who are yet able to balance their inner budgets and find
   available resources to sustain them
   in their trials and tribulations.
"The Spirit entered into me . . . and set me upon my feet,"
   cried Ezekiel while exiled in Babylon.
"The Lord is my Light and my Salvation; whom shall I fear?"
   exclaimed the psalmist.
"Take heart, men, for I have faith in God,"
   shouted Paul as he stood on the deck of a sinking ship.

Who are these characters who manifest such endurance in the
   face of terrifying odds?

They are simple men such as I,
   with like weakness, with the same passions,
   often afflicted by the same sins and failures,
   victims of many of the same circumstances.
What about these unbalanced, insolvent, defeated, expended
   hearts of my generation?
And what about my own inadequacies and fallibilities?

"Someone touched Me," said Jesus,
   "for I perceive that power has gone forth from Me."
But there are multitudes pressing up against the Christ.
They do so in the worship service, the Sacrament of the Altar,
   the preaching of the Word, the making of many prayers.
With their unnumbered needs they approach Him, crowd Him;
   yet the vast majority go their way
   with their needs unfulfilled,
   their hunger pangs unsatisfied, their chains unbroken.

I need not ask why.
The deliberate and decisive touch
   of the woman who approached Christ
   was the touch of faith,
   of utter confidence in His power to deliver and to heal.

It isn't enough to jostle Christ
   with noisy prayers and pious professions.
I must touch Him in faith.
I must continually be in touch with God.

+   +   +

*Loving God, I feel weak-kneed and heart-faint as I face the problems
and uncertainties of this day. Enable me to remain in touch with You
and to allow Your grace to turn my weaknesses into channels of power
and productivity. Amen.*

13

From Crisis
To Christ

"My God, My God, why hast Thou forsaken Me?" (Mark 15:34)

The agonizing inquiry of Christ on the cross has been moaned out
  by many in the midst of some terrible crisis in their lives.
It is the cry of millions who are oppressed
  and persecuted in this hour.
Multitudes throughout history, not finding an answer,
  have lived out their lives under that twisted question mark,
  making for themselves a hell on earth.
It was the cry of the psalmist:
  "O my God, I cry by day, but Thou dost not answer;
  and by night but find no rest."

It has been my cry during some of the dark hours in my life.
Whether the crisis be of my own making
  or the contribution of the chaotic world in which I live,
  a moment of excruciating pain or a period of despair
  forced me to probe the gray skies for some symbol of hope.

I do not always find deliverance from my dilemma.
I do find the grace and strength necessary for crisis living.
God will not always shelter me from the storms of life.
He does promise to keep me in those violent hours.
He stands by to sustain and to succor.
He is close enough to me to feel the suffering that I endure.

My great God does not scorn me for the cries of frustration
  and doubt that escape from my conflict-ridden soul.
He reaches out to touch me with healing,
  to endow me with strength.
My crisis may lead me into despair.
It is also capable of leading me to Christ.

"With the Lord on my side I do not fear," exclaimed the psalmist.
"In the world you have tribulation," said Jesus,

"but be of good cheer, I have overcome the world."
No matter what my crisis,
    Christ can and will meet it supernaturally.
It does not always resolve in total deliverance from the pain
    and anxiety of my hour of trial.
He does grant the grace to endure the same patiently,
    sometimes even joyfully.

The Christ who uttered the agonizing cry on the cross
    turned His crisis into confidence even while convulsed
    in pain and loneliness.
He quietly prayed:
    "Father, into Thy hands I commend My spirit."
He set before me the formula guaranteed to lead me from despair
    to hope, from darkness to light, from suffering to salvation.

He has forgiven and forgotten my past.
He stabilizes my present and secures my future.
He is even now preparing me for whatever crisis may come
    my way.

+   +   +

*Father, I commend my spirit and my hour of crisis into Your wise and
loving hands. Amen.*

Death Can Be Beautiful

**"Greater love has no man than this, that a man lay down his
life for his friends." (John 15:13)**

"It is appointed for men to die once," the Scriptures declare.
"What man shall live and never see death?" queried the psalmist.

I cannot entirely reduce its ugliness
   or minimize its horror.
I cannot forget my first childhood contact with it,
   nor the shock and pain of its brutal invasion
   of my family circle.
Despite the poet's attempts to picture it as a sweet slumber,
   or Forest Lawn's endeavors to glamorize it,
   the philosophers with their explanations,
   the preachers and their promises,
   there is a horror about death that strikes fear into my heart.

I cannot completely rid myself
   of its insidious threat to my being.
As surely as comes the end of summer,
   so surely must I face up to the fact of death,
   its parting of the ways,
   its incomprehensible darkness.

But faith does have an answer for this ultimate anxiety.
My Christ not only faced it, bluntly and biologically,
   He was victorious over it.
He transformed it from an enemy bent on my destruction
   into a friend that promises to usher me into eternal glory.
Thus death can be beautiful.
Its beauty is not only in its promotion to glory.
It can also serve a valid and worthwhile purpose on earth.

This was most certainly true in respect to the death of Christ.
It also holds true in respect to the deaths of Paul and Peter
   and James and the other apostles.
There are thousands who followed in their footsteps.
Their deaths were not always sudden or violent,
   but they were significant.
As the blood of the martyrs made fertile the soil
   for the growth of the church,
   so the deaths of unnumbered saints served to extend
   God's kingdom and to accomplish His purposes.
The passing of these beloved children
   served some purpose in history

and in some way benefited their brothers who continue
to walk in this discordant world.

This, then, is my concern —
    not that I shall die, for that I shall.
It is that I may die in God's place and in God's time.
I seek the grace to lay down my life for my brothers.
I pray that my passing will bring benefit and blessing
    to someone who follows behind.
Then, surely, even death can be beautiful.

+   +   +

*Great God, You who through Jesus Christ converted death from an enemy
into a friend, guide my footsteps in Your will for my life so that my passing
from this world may be at the right time and may in some way benefit
my brethren. Enable me even while I live to lay down my life for my fellowman. Amen.*

Consecrating
The Commonplace

**"Whether you eat or drink, or whatever you do, do all to the
glory of God." (1 Corinthians 10:31)**

I live with three- and four-inch headlines.
I think in superlatives.
I act in terms of what is the greatest, the most glamorous,
    the fantastic and the incredible.
The church today, unless it produces entertainment comparable
    to a television special,
    the glamor of a society debut,
    the mass appeal of a Billy Graham crusade,
    or the excitement of healing and holy-rolling,
    will seldom get a rise out of the man on the street.

Yet Christ's very first miracle, according to John,
was the transformation of water into wine.
He who refused to turn stones into bread
to satisfy His own hunger
did not hesitate to convert water into wine to further
the enjoyment of a crowd of merrymaking wedding guests.
Jesus persistently pointed up the splendor of little things.
He knelt to wash the feet of His disciples
and encourage them to wash one another's feet.
He commended the giving of a cup of cold water.
He commanded His servants to feed the hungry,
to clothe the naked,
to welcome the stranger,
to visit the sick and befriend the prisoner.
My great God has revealed that His glory and splendor,
His power and might
are available and applicable within the ordinary, routine,
mundane circumstances of everyday living.

It means that the commonplace task need no longer be common.
Whether it be in the realm of tedious housework
or laboring in a factory
or teaching a group of not-too-bright children,
the presence of Christ blesses and clothes it with
prestige and purpose.
He is able to work miracles in my most ordinary circumstances.
He can transform the day's drudgery and routine into vehicles
of blessing and abundance for me and for others about me.

My Lord, who came at Christmas, has come to manifest His glory
in even the most commonplace events of my daily routine.
He hallows every corner of my life with His perpetual presence.

+   +   +

*I thank You, O God, for the small things in life and for Your concern in
respect to the everyday routine of my existence. Bless these mundane hours
with Your miracle-working grace that they may reflect Your love and fulfill Your purposes. Amen.*

The Perils
Of Distraction

"You are anxious and troubled about many things." (Luke
10:41)

The pages of history are blood-smeared with the tragedies
of those who yielded to distraction.
From that first tragic distraction perpetrated by the serpent in
the Garden of Eden to the ear-splitting, head-spinning,
soul-tempting disturbances of modern living,
distraction reigns as king.

Martha was "distracted with much serving."
"You are anxious and troubled about many things," said Jesus.
I am also a victim of distraction.
The noise that accompanies urbanization,
bumper-to-bumper traffic, the high cost of living,
increased taxes, threat of war—
all this resloves in fear and frustration.
I am distracted by my own failures, victimized by my weaknesses,
threatened by the lack of tangible securities,
depressed by my inability to influence others.
I become anxious and troubled about many things.

He who diagnoses the disease
is also able to prescribe the remedy.
"Let not your hearts be troubled," said Jesus,
"Believe in God; believe also in Me."
"Have no anxiety about anything," wrote Paul,
"but in everything by prayer and supplication
with thanksgiving let your requests be made known to God."

"One thing is needful," Jesus said to Martha.
This is what He says to me.
I must look away from myself to God.

I must learn how to live in thankfulness.
I must lose my life in service for others.
I must commit my spirit into the hands of my heavenly Father.

There are men who say:
   "I believe in God Almighty, Creator of heaven and earth."
Many follow a different creed:
   "I believe in the almighty dollar,
   the necessity of financial security, the lust of the flesh,
   the importance of comfort, the desire for prominence,
   and in getting all I can out of life."
It is no wonder that men become victims of distraction.
Their souls become dry as dust, like wells without water
   or like the changing shapes of whirling storm clouds.
They seek for life's meaning in the grind of machinery,
   the advancement of science, or the thrill of the flesh.

"One thing is needful."
It is a day-by-day relinquishment of all that I am and have
   to Jesus Christ and to His purposes for my life.
Any other course in life would lead only to distraction.

+   +   +

O God, overwhelm my anxious and troubled heart with Your love and peace. Deliver me from distractions, and direct me to eternal rest and effective service in the center of Your divine will. Amen.

Mark of
A True Disciple

"By this all men will know that you are My disciples, if you have love for one another." (John 13:35)

"When you love your neighbor," said an old philosopher,
   "then you resemble God."

Love of brethren is the inevitable expression of true faith.
It is, according to my Lord,
the sole, sufficing evidence of an individual's Christianity.
Faith without this consequence would be no faith.
My neighbor is God's representative in this present,
sin-ridden world.
He is appointed by God to receive the sacrifices of love and
service which I offer to God through my neighbor.
As a Christian, I am a channel,
open upwards to heaven by faith
and outwards to my fellowman through love.
All that I possess has been received from God.
It has come by way of the lives and examples of fellow disciples
who loved me.
It is mine that I may pass it on to others.
I am called to be Christ to my neighbor.

"Even as I have loved you, that you also love one another,"
said Jesus.
But how can I love my neighbor as Christ loved me?
The springs of such love must be in God, not in me.
I must learn how to recognize Christ in my neighbor.
Even if my neighbor does not respond to such love,
it will at least flow freely in my soul.
It is truly a commandment, a standard,
an evidence of discipleship, that I love my neighbor.
It is also something that does not come naturally.
It is something I must be empowered to do, must learn to do.
It must begin right where I am, with those about me.
It is not easy.
It isn't even safe to love somebody.
There are hazards and risks involved.
To love at all is to be vulnerable.
It will mean that my heart will certainly be wrung.
It may possibly be broken.

There is an alternative.
I may lock myself in the casket of my own selfishness.

I would then never know the hurt of love rejected or spurned,
   or the pain and price of sharing myself with someone else.
But never to know God's love or to express that love to others
   is the shortest and most certain road to hell.

+   +   +

My loving Lord, enable me to manifest the mark of true discipleship and
courageously reach out in love to others. Amen.

Getting into
Deep Water

"Put out into the deep, and let down your nets for a catch."
(Luke 5:4)

"We toiled all night and took nothing."
This was Peter's response to his Lord's injunction.
It has often been mine.

I've honestly tried to serve Him,
   to build His church, extend His kingdom.
It often seems so ineffectual.
Trouble, sorrow, conflict, and weakness beset me on every side.
They constitute the facts of human nature and its environment.
I live them, eat them, sleep them.
They are here to stay.
The remarkable thing about it is that my Lord chooses that
   they remain.
He takes pains to get me to recognize and reckon with them,
   but He certainly does not remove them.
Perhaps He is attempting to teach me that I must not and need
   not deal with these things in the shallow waters of my own
   efforts and endeavors.

"Put out into the deep," Jesus said.
"Get out of the shallow waters of the apparent and the tangible,
  and push out into the depths of My reality,"
  He would say to me.
"You have only been dangling your toes at the shoreline of
  God's great sea of grace.
  Put out into the deep, and let down your nets.
  Soon you will be a catcher of men."
It is hardly possible to plunge from shore to ocean depths
  without first entering the shallows.
Shallow waters are necessary in my life.
The distressing things about me,
  the incapabilities within me
  must be a part of life's experience.
But they are only a means to an end,
  the shallow waters that precede the greater depths.
I must not settle for them or be overcome by them.
It is in the great, incomprehensible depths of God's reality
  that I will meet the supernatural.

Deep water is not something I should stay out of.
It is something I should get into.
By faith I must launch out
  into the depths of God's eternal grace.
There I will become effective in channeling the power
  and provision of God into the weakness and want ot humanity.

+ + +

*Great God, grant me the courage to break through the shallow waters
of human effort and launch my life into the great depths of Your grace.
Amen.*

My Name
Is Christian

"Holy Father, keep them in Thy name, which Thou hast given Me, that they may be one, even as We are one." (John 17:11)

My name is Christian.
It's a breathtaking truth to assimilate,
   a fabulous concept to comprehend.
I, sinful and self-centered, fallible,
   am appointed and empowered to be God's son and servant
   in this distorted world.
I am the very greatest of sinners,
   the least apt to deserve anything from God.
I have nothing within me worthy of His love and esteem.
Yet I am one of those whom He has chosen to carry out
   His purposes, to continue that which Christ began,
   to represent and reflect Christ to the milling multitudes.

My name is Christian.
It's an awesome, even terrifying truth.
What Jesus began in the three years of His visible presence
   He has appointed me to continue.
He set the example, got the ball rolling.
He reached out in self-sacrificing love to touch people in their
   need and to communicate to humanity the power of divinity.
Now He gives me direct access to His source of power and
   commands me to go out and perform even greater works than
   He did in the short time He was on this earth.

My name is Christian.
It's an upsetting, disturbing truth.
It means that I am not here to blow my own horn,
   to perpetuate my personal ambitions.
I am God's personal representative, His envoy,
   His son and servant, His disciple and priest,
   with the express assignment of dedicating

my very life to the carrying out of His purposes.
I am to be the channel and means of communicating His divine
    love and power into this disjointed humanity about me.
It means that I am no longer my own.
I am not free to go about satiating my own lusts.
I am free only to yield my freedom to Him
    and to others for His sake.
Until I do this, I am a disorbited being without essential
    meaning or purpose for my life.

My name is Christian.
It's a strange and solemn truth.
With Jesus no longer visibly present,
    I may be the only means God has of relating
    to those in my path.
They may never realize God or His claim on them
    except through me.

My name is Christian.
It's a very expensive truth.
It costs me everything I have.
I must deliberately choose to lose my life,
    deny self, renounce all that I have,
    and take up my cross to follow in the path of Jesus Christ.
I must do this not just once, but every day of my life.

My name is Christian.
It's an agonizing truth.
It underlines the depression and pain of failure
    and sends me daily to the Father's throne
    to claim anew His acceptance and forgiveness.
It identifies me with the pain and hurt,
    the emptiness and loneliness, the struggles and defeats,
    the poverty and deprivation of others.
When God's creatures suffer, God Himself suffers.
As a member of the body of Christ, I also must endure suffering,
    share in the suffering and sorrow of others,
    help bear their heavy burdens.

My name is Christian.
It's a truth far greater in value and worth
    than any human being can possibly conceive.
To be a son of God, claimed by His love,
    redeemed through His grace, empowered by His divinity,
    and guaranteed His eternal and abundant riches —
    all this is beyond one's wildest dreams.
All this is mine,
    for my name is Christian.

+   +   +

I thank You, O God, for adopting me as Your son and for appointing and empowering me to be Your servant. Grant to me the grace to be faithful to my new name and commission. Amen.

Only Sinners Are Eligible

"I have not come to call the righteous but sinners to repentance." (Luke 5:32)

"It is impossible for a man of himself to escape," said Seneca;
    "it must be that someone stretch forth a hand to draw him out."

God knows how I have sought for ways of escape.
There were times when I became so full up and fed up
    with life's bellyaches
    that I have wanted to go over the hill or hang one on.
Usually I took the route of frenzied activity
    or sensual indulgence.
I only discovered how impossible it was to run away from life's
    conflicts and problems.

It must be because the basis for such conflicts
    lies deep within me.
Wherever I go, I simply carry these distortions with me.
I may numb my sensitivity to them for a time,
    but they perpetually arise
    to confront me with renewed demands.
The seed for every distortion and weakness,
    for the darkness that surrounds me,
    the fears that distress me,
    the difficulties that overwhelm me,
    is rooted within my sin-permeated nature.
I simply cannot run away from that.
I was born out of orbit with God,
    at odds with His plan and purpose for my life.
My past failures, present complexities,
    even my fears for the future
    are part and parcel of this nature of mine.

There is only one antidote for the poison that taints my soul
    and binds me to the insufficiencies and inadequacies of this
    existence.
It is revealed in Jesus Christ and the Gospel He proclaims.
This Gospel tells me that Christ is after "the one who is lost."
Until I realize that I cannot escape, that I am lost,
    I am not even eligible for deliverance.
This is the very purpose of Christ's coming, the cross,
    the empty tomb, the churches of city and hamlet.
It is all for the purpose of receiving sinners.
Where there is no sin, no unsolvable problem, no overwhelming
    complexity, no moral or human weakness,
    there is no need of a Savior.

If I am up against something that is too much for me;
    if there are problems, weaknesses, sins,
    distortions in my life that I cannot solve or overcome;
    if I am lost in the wilderness
    of my own failures and insufficiencies —
    then I am eligible for the cure.

The Great Physician stands near to heal and deliver and forgive
and empower.
He will bring me into an experience of health and effectiveness,
strength and courage that will put point and purpose into
my life and living.

+   +   +

Great God, I am made of such frail stuff.
The very fiber of my being is restless and unsatisfied.
My every nerve reaches out for tangible thrill and sensual support.
Heaven seems so far off,
    if, indeed, it exists at all.
Your promises of joy and strength are vague, obscure, unreachable.
My sins accelerate; my faith shrivels.
I am simply not the stuff of which saints are made.
I feel empty and inadequate,
    and I cannot sense Your power or presence.

Is it possible that the saints of old felt the same way at times?
That they also were plagued with human weakness and frail flesh?
That they fell on their faces in foolish despair?
And yet their lives channeled Your strength.
Their words communicated Your Word.
Their deeds manifested Your love.
I hear so little about their defeats,
    but their victories are broadcast to every generation.

If You, O God, can turn my frail stuff into staunch material
    that can bless and benefit the lives of others,
    then, truly, You are a great God.

Under
New Orders

"Cast the net on the right side of the boat." (John 21:6)

The excitement had subsided.
The Christ who died on the cross had been raised from the dead.
But He was no longer with the disciples.
"I am going fishing," said Peter.
"We will go with you," responded the others.
Off they went to the routine business of making a living.

"But that night they caught nothing."
It summarizes so many of my post-Easter activities.
I basked in the joy and beauty of Easter.
I believed with all my heart that Jesus arose from the dead.
On Monday I was back at the salt mines.
It was business as usual,
    with the same defeats, anxieties, bondages
    as the week before.

A stranger appeared on the beach.
Following his orders the disciples recast their nets.
They immediately caught a huge quantity of fish.
"It is the Lord!" cried John.
Peter leaped out of the boat to meet his Master.
They learned that the resurrection was not
    the end of their lives.
It was the beginning.
They might go fishing again,
    but it would never be the focal point of their lives.
They were now the obedient, courageous, divinely inspired
    and empowered disciples of Jesus Christ.
And they would remain such until and beyond death itself.

This must be the answer to my lackadaisical, impoverished,
    insipid post-Easter existence.

It is the rediscovery of Christianity as a vital relationship
    with the living Christ.
Easter is not simply an annual festival.
It is an eternal fact that can inject divine power into
    my everyday circumstances.
The Christ that arose from the tomb must arise in my heart
    and there be permitted to reign supreme.
He must be accepted, appropriated, believed, and obeyed.

I have clung to His promises
    without fulfilling His prerequisites.
I have sucked Him into my private little club and selfish heart.
I have adopted and adapted Him to my formulas and routines.
I have reinterpreted Him to fit my notions.
And then I wonder why Easter makes no significant difference
    in my life and circumstances.

I must go back to my fishing nets,
    but I must return under new orders.
When I learn how to obey the principles and prerequisites
    of the living Christ,
    to allow Him to have His way in my life,
    the Christ of Easter will transform and empower me for
    post-Easter living.

+   +   +

*Eternal God, You who brought back Christ from the dead, resurrect
through Christ this poor spirit of mine. I do not seek to be delivered from
the daily drudgery of this workaday world. I pray that the Spirit of the
living Christ may be manifest in my everyday routine and activities. Amen.*

Loving
Is an Art

"Make love your aim." (1 Corinthians 14:1)

Loving is an art.
Any art, if it is to be mastered, demands knowledge, practice,
   and much effort.
An artist makes his specific art the primary concern of his life.
This is as true of love as it is of medicine or music or
   writing or acting.
It must be more important to me than anything else in life.
I must daily practice the art of loving.

It must be the consequence of my personal encounter with God.
If God through Christ loves, redeems, forgives, accepts,
   and keeps me forever,
      then how can I do anything else but accept others
      and thereby in some way transmit God's love to them?

But I am a human and fallible creature.
This necessitates intense effort in the art of loving.
It entails the will to love, the discipline needed daily
   to keep heart and mind set on loving.
It requires great concentration.
It demands much patience and understanding.
Courage is a requirement for those who would be proficient
   in the art of loving.
I may at times have to love in scorn of consequences.
Faith is essential, faith in God's acceptance of me, in His
   promises to me,
      and in His power to use me in reaching others and thereby
      demonstrating His love for them.
Tolerance is necessary in my acceptance of others.
I must cease to be judgmental or condemnatory.
I am not expected to condone wrongdoing.

I must sometimes tolerate it
   in my acceptance of people as persons.
I must love without the guarantee that those I love will respond
   or accept my love.

I walk precariously a taut tightrope,
      a thin razor-edge between the ideals of Christ and the
   weaknesses of humanity.
I know well the sickening imbalances,
      even the frightening failures that befall the sons of men.
I flirt with doubts in an era of intellectual pursuits
   and attainments.
I am plagued with inadequacies and inferiorities.
I am flattened by discouragement and besieged with despair.
I am tempted at times to quit the team and go over the hill.
But I listen to a Gospel that transcends the affections
   and afflictions of this existence.
I follow a Christ who calls me to a hard and narrow path.
I claim a grace that demands in turn
   my first love and allegiance.
I cling to the promises of ultimate deliverance and victory.
I will never be a paragon of virtue or an untarnished example
   of the life I proclaim.
I will fail in many things.
But God forbid that I fail to proclaim Jesus Christ, crucified,
      risen again, and ever present to love, accept, forgive,
      and lead men to eternal life and joy.
And God forbid that I ever cease to specialize in and concentrate
   on the art of loving.
This is the only way in which I can bring a loving God
   into encounter with love-starved souls about me.

+   +   +

*Loving God, teach me how to love. I am not capable of breaking through
my self-centered concerns. It is not really natural for me to give of myself
to others. But Your redeeming love has set me free to do just this. O Lord,
teach me how to love. Amen.*

The Blessing
Of Guilt

"If we confess our sins, He is faithful and just and will forgive our sins." (1 John 1:9)

I feel guilty.
It robs me of pleasant memories of the past.
It takes the joy out of the present.
It dims and obscures the future.
It is a constant thorn in the flesh that perpetually tumbles
    me from my pinnacles of happiness.
It is a cloud that is forever blotting out the sun.
It is a nagging demon that keeps me feeling
    inferior and inadequate.
No matter how carefully I tuck them away,
    there is always some skeleton rattling in my closet,
    some ugly Frankenstein that refuses to die.

It is not always the consequence of some evil thing I have done
    or some blooper I pulled.
Unworthy thoughts flash through my mind, and I feel guilty.
I meet someone who is bedridden, and I feel guilty because
    I am so healthy.
I read about the poor, and I feel guilty
    because I am so well off.
I even feel guilty about being happy
    when there are so many people about me who are unhappy.

Some of this guilt is necessary and potentially
    contributive.
Much of it is imaginary, repressed, or even unrecognized,
    with no actual basis or benefit.
But all of it must be dealt with lest it stifle
    my effectiveness or sap my strength
    or turn me into a raving maniac.

The burden of guilt is unbearable because it never was meant
   that I should bear it alone.
"There is therefore now no condemnation for those who are in
   Christ Jesus," wrote Paul the apostle.
Herein lies the cure for guilt.
There is no other remedy, nor is there need for any.

The conflicts of the Christian life emerge from this constant
   tussle with this body of sin and the guilt feelings that
   come from it.
The glory and joy of the Christian life
   lie in the fact that these conflicts
   keep me close to the grace of God that assures me that
   my sins are forgiven and my failures do not make me less
   valid or significant.

Guilt can be fraught with blessing.
It can prepare me for divine grace.
It is when I realize the significance
   of God's forgiveness and acceptance
   that I can turn in love and acceptance to my fellowmen
   and discover meaning and purpose
   in my daily conflicts and sufferings.

+   +   +

*Merciful God, may the feelings of my guilt, imaginary or deserved, drive
me to the facts of Your great act of reconciliation through Jesus Christ.
Enable me to lay hold of the blessed truth of my forgiveness and of my
validity and significance in Your eyes. Amen.*

Discipleship
Means Involvement

"As the Father has sent Me, even so I send you." (John 20:21)

"I just didn't want to get involved."
It was said by a man who stood by while a girl
    was brutally stabbed to death by some demented maniac.
There were thirty-seven other people
    who witnessed the same ugly tragedy.
They also did nothing.
They didn't want to get involved.

I wonder what I would have done if I had been there.
I do know that I haven't acted much differently
    toward the tragedies that transpire in the world about me.
I haven't manifested much concern about my politically oppressed
    brethren of the South,
    the enslaved millions behind the Iron Curtain,
    the starving masses in the Far East,
    even the people battered by pressures and beset by problems
    in the very next apartment.

I wonder if "noninvolvement" was the confession of many in that
    multitude that followed the hate-ridden murderers of Christ
    up to Calvary.

I cozy up to the kind of Christianity
    that is equated with plush pews and pious prayers,
    even if it involves an offering plate and a weekly pledge.
The kind demonstrated by Jesus Christ and reflected in His first
    followers is something I cannot comprehend.
I ignore it or relegate it to another age and bypass it.
I even find reason to criticize the occasional St. Francis or
    Schweitzer who do take our Lord's exhortations seriously
    and attempt to obey them in some realistic manner.

Discipleship means involvement.
Our Lord set the pace, and He expects His disciples to keep it.
He identified Himself with the agonies of mankind.
He became involved in their crying needs.
He even went so far as to bear the consequences of their sins.
To be a disciple of Jesus means that I
    who accept Him as my Savior
    must also accept Him as my Lord and Master.
To follow Him means that I continue in His course for my life.
I am expected not simply to criticize the distortions of humanity
    from the pews and pulpits of odd-shaped sanctuaries
    but to become involved in the blood and tears, the sorrows
    and sufferings of God's creatures in suburb and ghetto, alley
    and freeway, wherever they may be found.

Because I am involved in the sickness of my world,
    I must, as a disciple of Christ, become involved in its cure.
It will not be convenient or comfortable.
It might even be dangerous.
I may have to risk my reputation, wealth, status in society,
    my very life in this involvement.

But discipleship means involvement.
As my Lord suffered on my behalf,
    I am expected to suffer on behalf of others,
    to lose my life in service to them only to truly find it anew
    in the incomparable joy of being a priest and a servant of the
    living and eternal God.

+   +   +

Loving Christ, You who identified with me in my sins and sicknesses, adopted me as Your son, and commissioned me as Your servant, help me to fulfill my servanthood in identifying with the needs of my brothers and in communicating Your love and grace to them. Amen.

How to
Get Involved

"Go . . . I send you out as lambs in the midst of wolves."
(Luke 10:3)

I am well adjusted to that brand of Christian life
   that has centered on and is usually inclusive in
   congregations and institutions.
The rapid urbanization of society today is confronting me
   with problems and complexities that are forcing me
   to face up to what it really means to be the "salt of the earth"
   and the "light of the world."
It may be that I am being compelled to go back
   to the original commission of Christ
   and to His methods of carrying out that commission.

I am becoming aware that God is not confined to
   four-walled sanctuaries and church altars.
I delight to fellowship and commune and worship together with my
   Christian brothers and sisters in the local congregation.
Nevertheless, my most effective service for Christ
   must be carried on during my Monday-through-Saturday
   contacts with my fellowmen on the street, in the office, the
   classroom, the workshop, and the marketplace.

It is not difficult to be sincere, even enthusiastic, about
   my witness to those within the institution of the church.
But this makes no imprint whatsoever on the masses that inhabit
   the asphalt jungle or on the complex secular structures that
   formulate our policies and direct our activities.

Before I can communicate with the city,
   I must become involved with its people
   and its varied structures.
Before I can proclaim the Gospel,
   I must identify with people where they are.

The seventy disciples that Jesus sent out to precede Him were not
asked to sell door to door or to preach on street corners.
They were instructed to relate to people,
to become friendly with them,
to identify with them, listen to them, love them,
and share themselves with them.
They were to meet people and minister to them
at the point of their need.
"Heal the sick there," said Jesus.
Then, when the confidence of these people had been won, they
were to proclaim that the "kingdom of God has come near"
to them, that God was in their midst.

Maybe I need to become a "joiner,"
to single out those community programs and projects that are
seeking for human betterment and become involved with them.
Before I open my mouth, I had better cock my ears,
to listen and to extend my life in loving concern.
Sooner or later the opportunity will present itself for my
God-given proclamation and witness,
in deed if not always in word,
and I can represent Christ and demonstrate His love and
grace in ways I had never dared to imagine.

There may still be a place for street-corner revival meetings,
but involvement is necessary
if I am to reach the urban man for Christ.
There are dangers and risks.
I am like a "lamb in the midst of wolves."
But the Christian who doesn't get lovingly involved in the joys
and sorrows, the successes and failures of his fellowmen
isn't worth his salt and will certainly never become
the "salt of the earth."

+   +   +

*O Master, You have commanded me to "go." Tell me where to go and
how to channel Your healing and grace to the needy hearts of men all
about me. Amen.*

If I Have
A Spare Shirt

"He who has two coats, let him share with him who has none; and he who has food, let him do likewise." (Luke 3:11)

John the Baptist blasted away at the crowds with severe
    denunciations of their hypocrisy and fruitlessness.
They had faithfully performed their religious exercises
    and had proudly clung to their traditions,
        but they had about as much chance of becoming a part of
    God's kingdom as a dead fruit tree has of escaping the ax.

They were stripped naked under his scathing condemnations
    and were actually frightened.
"What then shall we do?" they asked.
John's reply was simple and to the point:
"The man with two shirts must share with him who has none."

I tend to relegate the Gospel According to John the Baptist
    to the realm of Old Testament obscurity.
I like the words of Jesus better, those words, at least,
    that appear to carry little threat to my awesome indifference
    to the needs of the masses about me
    or my apathy in the face of the inhumanity
    perpetuated on these masses.
I claim to "believe" in Jesus,
    make occasional visits to my religious shrine,
    and assume that this puts me in solid with God.

But every now and then I am brought up short
    with the fact that this "shirt-sharing" Gospel
    is as relevant to my theology as is the confession of sin.
It is also that aspect of the Christian life I assume I can cheat
    on without altering my relationship with God.

Jesus did not suggest that I could buy my way into His favor
   by participating in social welfare projects
   in poverty-stricken areas of some great city.
I am made His child by virtue of His gift of salvation,
   made available to me through His sacrifice on the cross.
At the same time He underlines the proclamation of John
   and makes it abundantly clear that genuine Christianity
   must resolve in "shirt-sharing."

I am enjoined to "preach the Gospel."
The fact is, there are times when the only way I can do this
   effectively is by way of sharing my shirts.
It is altogether possible that the number of shirts in my closet,
   my middle-class prosperity over against the vast multitudes
   of dispossessed, points up a fatal weakness in my faith.

+   +   +

*O God, forgive me my surpluses. Make me a steward over Your abundant
gifts to me and a channel through which they may reach the needs of my
brothers about me. Amen.*

Love
Or Perish

"He who does not love remains in death." (1 John 3:14)

The old poet insisted that "it is better to have loved and lost
   than never to have loved at all."
He could have been taking his cue from the apostle John,
   who intimates that not to love is to have lost already.

There are times when I am skeptical
   about this business of loving.
Maybe it is because I have reached out in tenderness only to
   get my knuckles rapped in scorn.

I tend to turn in all my emotional nerve endings
    and wall myself up with my own introversions.
It is like tucking oneself into a casket of self-idolization
    or self-pity.
It is a sort of living death that eats like a cancer
    at a person's vitals.

In order to love, I do have to gamble, to take a chance.
There are times when the one I love is not
    able to understand, receive, or assimilate such love.
Thus I am hurt and frustrated and cautious about extending
    my love to anyone else.
At the same time my very effort to love serves to stretch my soul
    and enlarge my capacity for enrichment.
At least I am alive when I reach out in love,
    whether that love is responded to or not.

Before I can love authentically and in scorn of consequences,
    I must realize and experience the love of God.
"By this we know love," wrote John,
    "that He laid down His life for us."
Then I must understand that love involves
    sacrificial living toward my fellowmen.
"We ought to lay down our lives for the brethren," said John.
This same writer goes on to point out that my love
    must be a matter of demonstration.
"Little children," he said, "let us not love in word or speech
    but in deed and in truth."
I must keep myself open to my brother's needs and become a line
    or channel of communication to the fulfillment of those needs.
The consequence ought to be that not only is his life enriched
    but my own life as well.

Love — and possibly get hurt.
Cease loving — and cease living.

+ + +

O God, You who have made known Your love for me through Jesus Christ,
enable me to break through the tentacles of self-centeredness and allow
You through me to touch others in love about me. Amen.

Immorality Within
The Church

"He who does not love his brother, whom he has seen, cannot
love God, whom he has not seen." (1 John 4:20)

I shun the traditional immoralities that incur the wrath of
God and church.
At the same time I am guilty of immorality
while basking within the blessings of church and social peers.

As guilty of immorality as the deviate who promotes illicit
relationships is the self-righteous professor of religion who
looks down his nose at another human being because his skin
is a different color.
When I, in attitude or action or even by neglecting to act,
deny another human being the equality, freedom,
respect, or dignity that I claim for myself, then I am immoral.

The strange and often shocking thing about it is that, whereas the
church has ascertained and proclaimed adequate dimensions
of Christian morality,
it has taken the less esteemed revolutionary movements
of secular society to point up how far I fall short
of my proclamations.

One of the more positive contributions
of the civil rights movement
is that it has backed me up against the wall with the demand
that I either put up or shut up.

I am discovering that my principles are often a far cry from
     Christ's prerequisites.
It is becoming increasingly clear that, if I am really going to
     be a Christian, I may have to get converted all over again —
     and this time in accordance
     with the love-God-love-your-neighbor standards
     that Jesus Christ laid down.

I fool myself if I think I can fulfill my responsibilities by
     simply searching my heart and declaring myself unbiased.
I had better adopt the kind of Christianity
     that will stand the test.
This is the kind that Christ offers and under which He invites
     me to serve.
If it doesn't result in loving acceptance of my fellowman
     regardless of race or creed
     and in sacrificial service to him whatever his need,
     then something is radically wrong with my Christianity.

I know that God accepts me even with my inborn bigotry,
     but He will not allow me to ignore it or whitewash it.
I must face up to prejudice and bigotry in my foolish heart.
I may not know how it got there.
I may never be completely rid of it.
I do know that I must deal mercilessly with it, for it cannot
     remain there unchallenged.

+   +   +

*Eternal God, blast out the bigotry and prejudice which threatens my
relationship to my fellowman and to You. Grant me the grace to manifest
to my brothers something of the love You have demonstrated to me. Amen.*

What Am I Trying to Sell?

"If we judged ourselves truly, we should not be judged. But when we are judged by the Lord, we are chastened so that we may not be condemned along with the world." (1 Corinthians 11:31-32)

I tend to become smug and self-sufficient in the "status quo" of
   some past experience or institutional achievement.
I neglect self-judgment.
Then it becomes necessary for the chastisement of God
   to take over.

I hear people making funny noises about the "death of God"
   or the dissolution of Christianity today.
Maybe I ought to listen to these voices from the secular world
   and try to understand them even if I cannot accept
   much of what these big mouths out of little men
   appear to be saying.

One thing they seem to say
   is that the large masses of our society
   will not hear God speaking to them
   through the same traditions and institutions
   that spoke to my grandparents and still speak to me.
Another thing they point out
   is that there are crass inconsistencies
   within orthodox Christianity as it is represented by many
   Bible-believing Christians and congregations.
When some of those who are most vociferous in preaching about
   God's love and man's need to love his neighbor are the most
   prejudiced opponents to integration,
   then it is little wonder that many sincere intellectuals lose
   faith in the institutional church.
These doubting, accusing, even scornful voices out of our world
   say something else I had better consider.
They spell out loud and clear

that in my concern for man's eternal welfare
I have often been guilty of neglecting his material,
mental, emotional, and physical welfare.
It is easy to shout "Amen!" to the proclamations of God's love
from the chancel and the pulpit.
It is not too difficult to preach about it in the town square or
on a street corner.
But it costs something to give up my spare shirt
to someone who has none,
to identify with and work for a minority race
seeking freedom and dignity,
to sacrifice a meal a day
so a starving child in India can eat for a week.

If this, even in some small measure,
represents the kind of Christianity that I have been selling,
it stands naked and exposed under the judgment of God.

When I leave my warm pew and truly begin to follow Christ,
it may mean, as it did with Jesus, that I will have to get my
hands dirty.
I may even discover, in my endeavors to be a servant of God,
that grace is not cheap,
that it costs something to be a Christian.

+ + +

Spirit of the living God, make me sensitive to the inconsistencies and contradictions of my life, and give me grace and wisdom in dealing with them. Help me to become truly authentic as Your son and servant in this discordant world. Amen.

The Importance
Of Being Imperfect

"My grace is sufficient for you, for My power is made perfect in weakness." (2 Corinthians 12:9)

Before I can accept the imperfections of others,
    I must learn how to accept my own.
I must not cherish them or condone them,
    but I certainly must recognize and be aware of them.
Some of them are cause for sorrow and shame,
    but even they do not subtract from my value and significance
    as a person.
It is the failure or inability to recognize, admit, and face up
    to them that gives these distortions the power to cripple me
    and render me ineffective as a man or a mate.

According to the wisdom of this world
    I am supposed to learn how to utilize my strong points
    of character to compensate for or to overcome my weak points.
According to the Gospel of Christ
    I am challenged to recognize and to allow my weaknesses to
    drive me to the supernatural resources of God, who promises
    to transform them into vehicles of divine power and grace.

The point is, my imperfections don't have to be my undoing.
They can be useful in directing me
    toward effectiveness and happiness.
But this will happen only if I have the courage to face them,
    accept them as a part of my sin-permeated human nature,
    and deal with them with my endowed intelligence and the
    grace made available to me in Jesus Christ.
I am aware of the diagnosis:
    "All have sinned and fall short of the glory of God."
How about the cure?
God's Word has the answer:
    "For by a single offering He has perfected for all time

those who are sanctified."
The perfection which God requires can never be a matter of
    personal achievement.
It is a gift.
Because it is a gift, it must be received as such.
I receive this perfection required of me
    not by personal effort or endeavor
    but by receiving Jesus Christ.

It's my imperfections that make me eligible
    for God's loving grace and the assurance of forgiveness
    as communicated to me through the Word and the sacraments.
It is His perfection that He shares with me as I respond in faith
    to His Word and sacraments.

+   +   +

*Eternal God, I thank You because there is no question as to my eligibility
for Your grace and forgiveness. I am a fallible human being, yet an object
of Your love and concern. Help me to give others the right to be imperfect,
and to offer them the kind of love and acceptance that You offer me. Amen.*

The God
Who Loves Failures

**"God has consigned all men to disobedience, that He may
have mercy upon all." (Romans 11:32)**

I know the meaning of failure.
Its consequences are reflected all about me.
Its insidious roots lie deep within me.
It permeates and taints my insides.
I can neither run nor hide from it.
I must resolve it in someone or something outside myself.

The psalmist also knew the meaning of failure.
"Save me, O God!" he cried,
  "for the waters have come up to my neck."
"He drew me up from the desolate pit, out of the miry bog,
  and set my feet upon a rock."

Failure must have been a part of Paul's experience.
"Wretched man that I am!" he wrote,
"Who will deliver me from this body of death?"
Even in the midst of despair and failure
  he knew the answer to his own question:
"Thanks be to God through Jesus Christ, our Lord!"

"I am unclean," was the admission of the leper to Christ.
It was one of the prerequisites for being made clean.
"I am unworthy," confessed the centurion.
It was the beginning of a great miracle in his life.
"I acknowledged my sin to Thee," cried David.
"Then Thou didst forgive the guilt of my sin."

I have failed.
It could be the threshold to success.
It is the fact of failure that slays self-sufficiency and
  prepares me for faith.
It is faith in the grace and power of God through Christ that
  introduces me to a life of effectualness.

I am acceptable to my God, for my God loves failures.
He can accomplish His purposes in my life in spite
  of my failures.
It is His miracle-working power that can turn my failures
  into successes.

+   +   +

Eternal God, I acknowledge and confess my failures. Grant me Your forgiveness. Keep them from hurting anyone else. Bring forth out of the ugliness of my faults and failings the beauty and joy of Your will for my life. Amen.

The Right
To Be Happy

"These things I have spoken to you, that My joy may be in you and that your joy may be full." (John 15:11)

Do I have the right to be happy?
Materialistic philosophy responds in the affirmative.
Our commercial world boldly advertises the products guaranteed
   to contribute to such happiness.

The Christian philosophy is not so optimistic about it.
It rather celebrates the act of giving up or denying personal
   happiness in favor of someone else's happiness.
One of the strange paradoxes of Christianity is that its promise
   of eternal joy may entail temporal unhappiness.

It almost seems as if my pursuit of happiness
   drives it further away.
It is as elusive as a fox in a field
   and as impossible to latch onto
   as a taxicab on a rainy night.
And it is true more often than not
   that my pursuit of temporal and tangible happiness
   endangers the happiness and well-being of others.
When I snatch at that which I assume will make me happy,
   it often results in hurting or taking away from someone else.

I may not have the right to be happy.
If such happiness is designed to satiate my ego or pacify
   my self-centered nature,
   I can hardly, as a Christian, claim that right.
But I do have the right to joy.
I do not merit it, but God offers it.
Nowhere and at no time has God promised sensual happiness,
   but His Word is full of promises of joy.

The receiving of such joy may well include the denial of
   personal happiness.
This kind of self-denial is never easy.
It is not practiced for the purpose of pleasing God.
It is necessary to deny or sacrifice some of the natural and
   beautiful delights around me in order to prepare my heart
   for the best that God has for me
   and to channel His joy and accomplish His purposes
   in my life and in the lives of others about me.

As a Christian, I don't have the right to be happy
   if the acquisition of such brings unhappiness or hurt
   to someone else.
I do, because of God's grace, have the right to joy.
Even in the midst of unfulfilled desire and pain,
   I can discover the peace and joy
   of a right relationship with God
   and the out-of-this-world enrichment
   that comes with communicating His joy to others in my path.

+ + +

*Gracious God, forgive me for confusing happiness in satisfying myself
with the joy You give me in Christ. Fill me with the faith that finds joy
in Christ even when my desires are unfulfilled and pain troubles my
heart. Amen.*

*Love, Honor
And Forgive*

**"If you do not forgive, neither will your Father who is in
heaven forgive your trespasses." (Mark 11:26)**

I never cared for that old marriage vow that read: "Love, honor,
   and obey."
I think it ought to read: "Love, honor, and forgive."

It is possible that the word "love" ought to be
  eradicated altogether from our vocabulary.
It has come to mean so much more, or less,
  than what it was designed to mean.
At any rate, "love" in its original and more accurate connotation
  certainly must include the ability and willingness to forgive.
Human love, which is essentially a reflection of divine love,
  is not really love at all unless it is a forgiving love.
I am full of poetry and music toward my fellowmen
  as long as their affections and activities pamper my ego.
This can hardly be construed as love.

"Love, honor, and forgive."
It must begin with my acceptance of God's incomprehensible love
  and forgiveness.
It must be followed — and this is implied in such acceptance —
  by my ability to forgive myself.
It is remarkable how often
  my unforgiving attitude toward others
  is in reality a reflection or a projection
  of my disgust with myself.
A humble and honest appraisal of myself should certainly make me
  tender, acceptive, understanding,
  and forgiving of my fellowmen.
It doesn't mean that I condone their failures and distortions
  any more than I am expected to condone my own.
But I may have to learn how to tolerate the weaknesses they have
  not learned how to transform into strength,
  the liabilities they have not yet turned into assets.
I need to accept them as valid, significant, worthwhile persons.
As children of God they are just as close to Him as I am,
  and just as continually in need of His grace.
They belong to the same club as I do,
  the brotherhood of sinners saved by grace.
One prerequisite for membership is that
  through the loving acceptance of one another
  we contribute to the sanctification of the others,
  and we grow together into vessels and vehicles of usefulness
  and effectiveness.

I must be aware that my forgiveness of my fellowman
   needs to be genuine.
It is so easy to adopt a facsimile of the real thing,
   a condescending, holier-than-thou sort of attitude.
True forgiveness is not a degrading or demoting
   of the person concerned,
   taking away his stripes or reducing his rank.
Forgiveness is acceptance of the person concerned as one's equal,
   a brother or sister in Christ.

"Love, honor, and forgive."
It is essential to happy and fruitful
   interpersonal relationships.
It is possible only by the grace of God.

+   +   +

You have seen my sin, O God, and have forgiven me. Now enable me to demonstrate my gratitude in loving acceptance of my fellowman irrespective of his failures and faults. Amen.

Blessed Are
They Who Struggle

"We rejoice in our sufferings, knowing that suffering produces endurance." (Romans 5:3)

I used to envy those people for whom sainthood appeared to come
   so easily.
They were undaunted by the weaknesses of the flesh and
   untouched by the wickedness that surrounded them.
They manifested a sort of out-of-this-world aura that immunized
   them to the plagues and pitfalls of this chaotic world.
Their halos sat firmly on their heads even when the world was
   falling apart about them.

But as I grow older,
   my youthful envy turns into tolerance and sympathetic concern.
"Be kind," said an old sage, "for everyone you meet is fighting
   a hard battle."
Indeed, the person who has no conflict in life would be the one
   to be pitied.
He must be a part of a cocoon existence that is immersed in
   false comfort or fat-bellied contentment.
He would not be likely to make much of a contribution to the
   welfare of humanity.

Thus I continue to struggle.
And where there is struggle,
   there is bound to be a measure of failure.
This is true whether it is the struggle to gain knowledge,
   explore outer space, or keep pace with Soviet rearmament.
It is true in the moral and spiritual nature of man as well.
But the element of failure has been foreseen and accounted for
   through the redemption of Jesus Christ.
As a matter of fact, His divine forgiveness and acceptance
   is applicable only where there is failure.

Blessed are they who struggle, for they shall become strong.
The tragedy is not with failure
   but with the cessation of struggle.
Whatever form the enemy of my soul may assume,
   I must continue to do battle with him.
If I fail—and I will at times—
   I must claim God's forgiveness and rise to fight once more.
If I remain sensitive to divine leading
   and receptive to divine enablement,
      I shall by divine grace become stronger through my struggles
      and shall live to claim eternal victory.

+   +   +

*Great God, teach me how to find a measure of joy and contentment and
achievement even in the midst of my struggles. Amen.*

Life's
"Little Whiles"

"A little while, and you will see Me no more; again a little while, and you will see Me." (John 16:16)

I exist in the "little while" of Christ's absence.
It is often a time of sorrow, loneliness, and darkness.
The love and concern of a heavenly Father is not always
    comprehensible to my physical senses.
The vision of Christ, at times so real and fulfilling,
    turns into cold, gray skies, unanswered prayers, and
    unsatisfied longings.
There are times when I find myself doubting the very existence
    of a loving God.

"What does He mean by 'a little while'?"
    asked the disciples among themselves.
They were soon to find out.
Jesus, their Bright Star and Supreme Hope,
    their Love and their Joy,
    was brutally torn from them and put to death.
They had forsaken business, profession, families—
    all to follow the Christ.
And now all was gone.

And then, just a few hours later,
    the whole sky was ablaze with new light.
These grief-stricken hearts were possessed with a new joy.
Sorrow had been transformed into vibrant gladness.
Their "little while" of darkness burst into the dawn of a
    new and glorious day.
God does not create these "little whiles" of darkness.
He does allow them to come my way.
"So you have sorrow now," said Jesus,
    "but I will see you again, and your hearts will rejoice."

I may never discover His total purpose for these hours of
   confusion and difficulty,
      but I would never surrender my rebellious will back to God
      if there were no dark hours to bring me to the end of my rope
      and the realization of my need of Him.

The "little while" of darkness is by no means a "little while"
   of Christ's absence.
"It is the Lord who goes before you,"
   said Moses to the Israelites;
      "He will be with you, He will not fail you or forsake you."
Nor will I be forsaken by God.
I may not sensually apprehend His presence,
   but He indwells His every disciple
   and strengthens, comforts, and guides His every child.

I need not shun or fear the "little whiles" that plague my life.
I need only learn how to use them to develop my faith
   and to sharpen my discernment of spiritual values.

+   +   +

*Ever-present God, may the hours of despair and emptiness in my life
drive me always to the fountainhead of Your eternal grace. Amen.*

Stop Fretting!

**"Fret not. . . . Be still before the Lord, and wait patiently for
Him." (Psalm 37:1, 7)**

This is a great day for fretting.
The masses of my world appear to be farther from God than they
   have ever been.
The organized church is losing its once-important status in the
   Christianized segments of our world.

The heart of man created to harbor God has become focused on
    innumerable finite philosophies and religions.
The frightening distortions that permeate all facets of society
    are but symbols of man's ever-growing estrangement from his
    Creator and Redeemer.

I need to be reminded of very simple truths:
    that God is still God,
    that the victory over evil was won by way of the cross and
    the empty tomb,
    that His purposes are being fulfilled and will be consummated
    in His own good time.

I recognize that some of the old traditions that I have honored
    and loved no longer have much validity.
The symbols that mean so much to me may no longer have
    meaning to the multitudes about me.
Even the institutions that directed me to God are beginning to
    take on new shapes and forms.
But the vacuum in men's hearts and the God who can fill that
    emptiness remain forever the same.
"Jesus Christ is the same yesterday and today and forever,"
    asserts the New Testament.
"I will not fail you or forsake you,"
    said the Lord.

It is becoming less popular and probably more difficult for me
    to be a Christian.
The fellow travelers of nominal Christianity are falling off.
The men are being separated from the boys.
But for those who are dedicated and determined followers
    of Jesus Christ, the present era and the years to come
    will be the most challenging the church has ever known.

Thus I must stop fretting.
God is here among us.
He continues to be my Refuge and Strength.

"Relax," He would say to me,
  "and remember that I am still your God;
  and I still hold the reins on this world of yours."

+ + +

Forgive me for fretting, loving Lord, and give me the courage to demonstrate Your love and fulfill Your purposes in a world that tries so hard to ignore You. Amen.

Maybe My God
Is Too Small

"Unless you eat the flesh of the Son of Man and drink His blood, you have no life in you." (John 6:53)

Our Lord performed the feeding-the-five-thousand miracle.
Impressed with such remarkable activity,
  the masses pressed upon Him,
  not in loving worship but in curious speculation.
What a king He would make!
They would never go hungry.
He would supply all their needs and wants.
This kind of Christ they would gladly follow.

Jesus set about to undermine these ridiculous concepts
  concerning Himself.
He attempted to point up their true need,
  the need of restoration and reconciliation to God.
He had come to fulfill that need.
By receiving and loving and following Him they would discover
  the food and fulfillment that eternally satisfies.

They were not capable of comprehending spiritual truth.
They lived by their stomachs.

Such talk did nothing to satiate their natural appetites.
They left Christ for more profitable pursuits.

I understand far more about Christ's person and purposes
    than did this speculating crowd.
But it may be that my God is still too small.
I attempt to confine Him to my little formulas and pet schemes.
I accept as much of Him as serves my selfish interests.
I still need to learn the meaning of "eating His flesh"
    and "drinking His blood."
Perhaps it means that it is not enough to accept His forgiveness
    or His promise of eternal life.
He does not offer Himself for the sole purpose of making me
    feel safe and secure.
To "eat" and "drink" Christ dramatizes my need of becoming
    identified with Him,
    of making Him an integral part of my being,
    of uniting totally with Him and His purposes.

It also means, my union with Christ,
    that I who eat of the Bread of Life
        must become broken bread to the hungry lives of men about me.
I who live by His divine sacrifice am to offer up my life
    as a sacrifice on the altar of my fellowman's need.

If I am simply professing Christ, fleeing to Him,
    screaming out my agonies at Him when the road gets rough,
    then my God is too small.
I must do this at times, but I must do far more.
I must receive Christ as He is, in all that He is,
    as He declares Himself to be.
I must be His totally, intimately, with all that I am and have.
It is only then that God can become large enough within me
    to do something for me and through me.

+   +   +

*Forgive me, O God, for trying to use You as I try to use others in order
to pad my ego or to pacify my anxious and insecure heart. Lead me, in*

scorn of consequences, into the intimate depths of authentic discipleship.
May You truly be a great God in me and through me. Amen.

The Crucible
Of Conflict

"When you pass through the waters, I will be with you; and through the rivers, they shall not overwhelm you. . . . For I am the Lord, your God." (Isaiah 43:2-3)

I am involved in conflict — fierce, vicious, unabated.
It is the law of all nature.
Life is transmitted through struggle and travail.
It is thus that a mother gives birth to a child.
Conflict is a constant ingredient in the child's development.
From the day of breast-weaning to his first day in school,
    from his struggle for learning through the day-by-day,
    hand-to-mouth existence in a competitive world,
    conflict is perpetually present.

This conflict is apparent in my moral and spiritual nature.
Where there is conflict, there is the possibility of defeat.
The tragedy is not in an occasional defeat;
    it is in the cessation of struggle,
    the refusal to face up to conflict.

I have prayed for deliverance from a particular conflict.
The conflict only became more intense.
God did not promise to rescue me from life's struggles.
He did promise to keep me whole and safe amid them.
He does not shield me from the pains of my many wounds.
He does enable me to bear them.
Thus I must live daily within the crucible of conflict.
I must learn how to live effectively amid struggle,
    how to turn my many failures into occasional successes,
    how to develop and mature amid the throes of battle.

Conflict is necessary in the life of God's servant.
It purges and prepares him for productive service.
It is on the battlefield of life that he can minister to the
wounded and fallen about him.
God has no way of touching suffering humanity save through His
servants who are immersed in humanity's conflicts.

God may not calm the forces and gales that beat around me,
but He can calm the storm that rages in my heart.
He is with me even as I pass through the cascading rivers
and burning fires of this earthbound life.
He is with me in the midst of my conflicts.

+   +   +

O God, You know my conflicts. You know of my many defeats. You know how incapable I am of fighting my battles alone. Grant me the grace to endure, to mature, and to manifest loving concern for my brethren as we struggle through life together. Amen.

When One Feels Like Nagging

"Judge not, that you be not judged." (Matthew 7:1)

Sometimes I feel like nagging.
Most often it appears as slicing, deprecating jibes,
a belittling, unappreciative attitude toward the other
person's character or contributions.

What is so disconcerting is that it is usually not the
incompetence of my victims that makes me so critical
toward them.

It is often some disturbance or distortion within myself.
It is a kind of projected form of self-depreciation.
Because I feel small, inferior, invalid, and inadequate,
    I find myself hacking away at somebody else
    until he is demoted to my assumed dimensions
    or until I can feel that I stand taller.

What can I do about it?
I can force myself to say only nice, appreciative things
    about others.
This is the least I can do—but it is not enough.
It is like applying vaseline to the abdomen when an appendectomy
    is really called for.
Control is commendable, but sometimes cauterization is necessary.
I must find ways and means of facing up to myself, of handling
    effectively, even if they can't be totally overcome,
    these inner distortions of mine,
    lest they spring forth to injure others as well as myself.

It doesn't happen overnight.
It begins with my acceptance of myself as God accepts me.
And this acceptance is not dependent on the positive
    or deterred by the negative potentials of my life.
God through Christ has lovingly embraced me and reinstated me
    as a member of His family.
I am important to Him—along with all of His frail,
    fallible children.
If I can really believe in God's acceptance of me,
    then I will be less critical of my human counterparts.

I must try to understand that when I criticize others who are
    struggling to acknowledge their status
    as persons of worth and value
    I may be kicking someone who is already down,
    and doing irreparable harm.
"Let him who is without sin among you
    be the first to throw a stone at her,"
    said Jesus concerning a woman who was caught in the act.

May God's love and mercy for me cause me to drop my stones
and be loving and merciful and tolerant in turn.

+ + +

*O God, while I must be critical in respect to many of my attitudes and
actions, teach me how to be generous and kind in my consideration of
my fellowmen. Amen.*

Go and
Wash Feet

**"If I then, your Lord and Teacher, have washed your feet,
you also ought to wash one another's feet." (John 13:14)**

I had been brought up to believe that, for the Christian,
    service to humanity meant verbal proclamation.
I know I cannot ignore Christ's command to "preach the Gospel."
What makes me think I can ignore His command to "wash feet"?

What my Lord seems to be saying is:
    "This is what it means to love your fellowman, your neighbor,
    as yourself. It means not simply your condescending
    willingness but your eagerness to stoop to the humblest
    act of service on his behalf. This is what I have done
    in descending from heaven to stoop to your needs,
    in shedding the glory and power of divinity
    to become identified with your humanity.
    Now this is the manner in which you
    are to carry on My ministry. You are to meet your fellowman
    in loving concern and in utter humility at his point of need."
It is difficult for me to consider foot-washing important
    in comparison to proclaiming the Gospel.
Yet here it is, my Lord's command to wash feet,
    to serve the needs of men,

to expend my life and energies on behalf of others.
This humble act of foot-washing is communication of another sort,
    and it sets up lines of communication
    over which the Gospel may ultimately be proclaimed.
If I cannot comprehend the point of Christ's example,
    I may never really discover the joy and meaning and purpose
    of redemption.
After all of Christ's exhortations and demonstrations
    and the examples of scores who followed Him,
    I am still inclined to confine my religion
    to a set of spiritual exercises
    that I carry on in prayer closet or church sanctuary.
As long as I do this, I am still just about as self-centered
    as those who have never heard about Jesus Christ,
    and this in spite of my constant exposure to the Gospel,
    my professions of faith in the Christ,
    and my professional attempts to proclaim Him to others.

I am born to be a servant.
If I am truly to serve Christ, I may have to begin by washing
    another's feet,
    by engaging in a most humble and unspiritual act
    of loving service to the person closest to me
    or the neighbor next door.
If I refuse to be a servant, I shall live and die as a slave,
    a slave to self-centeredness,
    from which I have never allowed Christ to set me free.
I have asked Christ to set me free.
I have claimed His redeeming power for that purpose.
If I am truly to discover that freedom,
    I must act as a creature of freedom,
    as one who has been set free in order to live for others.

+   +   +

*Lord and Master, You who left heaven's majesty to stoop to my earthbound
nature in order to meet my needs, grant me the kind of love for my fellowman that will tear down the barriers of pride and self-concern and enable
me to meet him at his point of need. Amen.*

Courage
To Live

"Let not your hearts be troubled, neither let them be afraid."
(John 14:27)

"God grant me the serenity to accept things I cannot change,"
  begins a popular prayer.
I am aware of the need of courage to change the things I can.
The greater part of my life is supposedly dedicated
  to that proposition.
What I must become increasingly aware of as I face humanity's
  distortions within me and about me is the need of courage
  as well as serenity to accept the things I cannot change.

Physical illnesses, emotional defects, moral failures,
  personality weaknesses—that which can be changed must be
  changed lest it destroy me or others about me.
But there are some things that the facilities of medicine,
  psychology, and religion cannot alter, things from which my
  great God Himself apparently withholds deliverance.

What I am not delivered from I must learn to live with.
As I must accept and live with my human fallibility,
  so I must accept and live with some of the perpetual
  symptoms of that fallibility.
I cannot run away from it or sweep it under the rug
  or fence it about with vain rationalizations.
I can face up to it, recognize that it does not subtract from
  my validity before God or man,
    and enlist divine grace to keep it from hurting others or
    hindering me from working within God's purposes.

As a matter of fact, I can use it.
"My power is made perfect in weakness," said the Lord to Paul.
With this revelation he received the courage and the grace to be
  "content with weaknesses."

I may never find this kind of contentment,
   but my "thorn in the flesh" may be useful in keeping me close
   to God and humbly dependent on Him
   for my daily ration of grace.
It may also serve to make me more loving and accepting toward
   others whatever their pains and problems may be.
That suffering which I cannot change or from which I may
   never be delivered, though not intended by God,
   is often permitted by God and can be used by God, who will
   thereby enable me to fellowship with others who suffer and
   bring to them the comfort of a loving God.

+   +   +

*Eternal God, grant me the courage to live in spite of and even in the
midst of those things I cannot change. May these ever-present thorns
goad me in the direction of Your will for my life, and may they mellow
and soften me in my concern for others. Amen.*

When There's Meaning in Misery

**"Though I walk in the midst of trouble, Thou dost preserve
my life . . . and Thy right hand delivers me." (Psalm 138:7)**

The most atrocious and destructive type of suffering is pain
   without purpose, misery without meaning.
My suffering becomes critical
   not in the physical hurt it inflicts
   but in my inability to discover any logical reason for it.
I can endure the dentist's drill because I know its objective.
But when some hideous accident befalls me or my loved ones,
   the unreasonable waste and purposelessness of it haunts me
   with excruciating agony.

Suffering that has meaning is endurable,
no matter how intense the pain or how deep the hurt.
But the meaning of suffering cannot be ascertained
by any logical means.
It cannot be diagramed or computed.
It transcends man and human reason.
Thus I must look beyond the material or physical dimensions
of life for such meaning.

The Christian faith offers such meaning and purpose.
It asserts that though God does not intend my sufferings,
He involves Himself in them.
He has done this through Christ, who suffered on our behalf
and is able to "sympathize with our weaknesses."
It is His presence in my trials and conflicts that truly does
give meaning and purpose to them.
"In the world you have tribulation," said Jesus.
At the same time He guaranteed ultimate victory.
He who turned the defeat of the cross into the victory of
the empty tomb has made available His power to work
similar miracles in my life.
My misery, be it physical pain or personal failure,
is not the end of life.
It is more likely its beginning.
As the struggles and defeats of history
were necessary to its successes,
so are the failures and frustrations of my life.
No one is immune to suffering.
Nor does my God offer to absolve me of it as long as I am
on this earth.
But if I can truly commit myself into the hands of my loving
God, I will find the grace to endure suffering gracefully,
for it then assumes some meaning and purpose
and may well become the basis
for self-enrichment and service.

+ + +

O God, I felt Your loving presence today.
There was no ecstatic dream or dazzling vision.
Nor did I speak in strange tongues
     or see Your finger writing across the night.

Yet it was as if Christ Himself
     broke into my cloud of despair
     and touched me with divine concern
     and supernatural power.

And thus Christ did come to me today;
He came by way of a friend.
He is a very dear friend
     who grieves with me in my failures
     and rejoices in my victories.

He put his arm around me today
     and assured me of his love and concern for me.
Though he never pries into my secrets,
     he somehow feels my hurt
     and senses my frustration.
Today, when I needed Your precious touch,
     he was there to transmit it.
In his love I felt Your love;
In his concern I realized Your concern.

I thank You, God, for my friend.
He was Your messenger to me in a time of need.
Enable me to be such a friend to him,
     and to others in their hour of pain or loneliness.
And may I be as eager to walk with them in their defeats
     as to applaud them in their successes.

He
Does Care

**"I am the Good Shepherd; I know My own, and My own know
Me . . . and I lay down My life for the sheep."** (John 10:14-15)

"No man cares for me," agonized the psalmist on one of the
blue Mondays of his life.
The statement is attributed to David and was spoken
while he was hiding from King Saul in a dark cave.
There are caves along my sojourn through life,
and I duck into one of them now and then to hide from
something that frightens or threatens me.
And there I moan out my loneliness and despair,
telling myself lies about the Divine's indifference
and my fellowman's unconcern about my problem.

I may have reason for doubting my fellowman's concern about me.
He is often too preoccupied with his own failures or successes
to coddle me in my confusion and confoundment.
It is true that God's love,
usually transmitted by way of men who have encountered Him
and are dedicated to manifesting and communicating Him,
is often made ambiguous by human insensitivity.

But over and above the fallibility of human beings
is the perpetual and eternal truth
of God's love and concern for me.
"Cast all your anxieties on Him, for He cares about you,"
wrote Peter.
There are times when the arm of faith must reach over and around
the apparent lack of human concern into the very heart of God.
I can read the message of that bleeding heart
in His precious Word:
"I know My own, and My own know Me . . . and I lay down
My life for the sheep."

Even David had to conclude again and again:
"He delivered me because He delighted in me."

It's high time I emerge from my sorry little cave of morbidity
and self-pity and find my place in the human stream of this
workaday world.
Maybe I can even demonstrate my faith by expressing love
and concern for others.

+   +   +

O God,
How full of wonder and splendor You are!

I see the reflections of Your beauty and hear the sounds
    of Your majesty wherever I turn.
Even the babbling of babes and the laughter of children
    spell out Your name in indefinable syllables.

When I gaze into the star-studded sky
And attempt to comprehend its vast distances,
I contemplate in utter amazement my Creator's concern for me;
I am dumbfounded that You should care personally about me.

And yet You have made me in Your image.
You have called me Your son.
You have ordained me as Your priest
    and chosen me to be Your servant.
You have assigned to me the fantastic responsibility
    of carrying on Your creative activity.

O God,
How full of wonder and splendor You are!

Eating
Humble Pie

"The sacrifice acceptable to God is a broken spirit; a broken and contrite heart, O God, Thou wilt not despise." (Psalm 51:17)

The way to God is the way of humility.
The way to humility is the way of a broken heart.
"The Lord is near to the brokenhearted," said the psalmist,
"and saves the crushed in spirit."

It has always been so.
When God comes near, men's hearts are broken.
Moses, the one-time prince and contender for the throne of Egypt,
    judged himself as an incapable fool when God came near.
Gideon was the smallest of his family in the tribe of Manasseh
    when God came near.
Isaiah was struck to the ground in fear-ridden confession
    when God revealed Himself.
From Abraham, the father of Israel,
    to the insignificant tax collector
    beating his breast in the temple,
    the sign and seal of God's presence has always been brokenness.

This has been true in my life.
When God came near, I found nothing in myself to cling to.
My aims and ambitions were transformed into gaping idols.
My merits and manners became dead leaves before the wind.
My sins and shortcomings blotted out the very sun.

Before I can be of use to God,
    I must be broken, crushed,
    sometimes even to the point of despair.
There may be some people who enter into this experience in almost
    imperceptible ways, under the preaching of the Word,
    the prick of the conscience.
Others need to be hit by a truck or frightened by an earthquake

or drained dry by some physical disease or emotional upset.
I am numb and thick-skulled.
The Spirit must often use drastic means
    to break me and to ready me for reclamation and
    reconsecration.
Only then will I break up,
    recognize my fallibility and insufficiencies,
    and humble myself before Almighty God.

If I am confounded by conflict and cowed
    by the circumstances about me,
    undressed and beaten down by life's innumerable tragedies
    and human nature's insurmountable problems,
    the soil of my heart is made fertile for the experience of
    God's supernatural love and grace.
The Divine Potter reaches out to gather together
    the broken pieces and transform them into a vessel
    that will be beautiful and precious in His eyes.
The way of the broken heart is the way to God.
It is also the way to true significance and worth.
"The sacrifice acceptable to God is a broken spirit."

+   +   +

*O great God, I am a very little man. I have nothing in myself that is pleasing
to You. I continue to submit all that I am and have to Your breaking and
purging. Be gentle, O God, and make out of the pieces of my life something
that will glorify Your name and serve to accomplish Your purposes. Amen.*

Temptation

**"Because He Himself has suffered and been tempted, He is
able to help those who are tempted." (Hebrews 2:18)**

Temptation!
For many on Main Street it's a trade name
    for a seductive perfume.

For the playfully casual it's a mischievous smirk under tall hat
    and short horns.
For the daring man of the world it's an invitation
    to win another medal.
For the perpetual failure it's the prelude to another defeat.
For the aspiring but struggling Christian it ought to be a call
    to arms — or the eerie scream of a nearly spent shell
    that sends him clawing into the ground for shelter or support.

Only too often it takes the shape of bread that promises
    to satiate my hunger, or water to slake my thirst.
It promises fulfillment, happiness, poking into my dark hours
    with beckoning fingers of hope and light,
    interrupting my drudge-laden routine with moments of
    tantalizing excitement, relieving my pain with experiences
    of pleasure and delight.

And it never lets up.
I almost envy my Lord, who had angels to succor Him after His
    forty-day ordeal in the wilderness.
I often wonder if it's fair that I, composed of such human stuff,
    should be so constantly exposed
    to that which cannot be humanly resisted.

But I am exposed.
I discover very realistically that I simply cannot win them all.
I have been told that temptation is necessary
    to Christian maturity.
I must not seek it, nor do I need to.
It is amply provided around every corner of my earthly sojourn.
It can be used by God to develop dependence on Him.
It ought to resolve in keeping me close to Him.
I am supposed to grow stronger in the heat of conflict,
    discovering my weaknesses to be channels of divine power and
    sustenance.

God doesn't send temptation, but He does allow it.
And with every temptation He has promised the grace to resist it.
I must learn how to tie on to that grace.

+ + +

Lord, I've failed again.
Despite my firm resolutions and determined efforts
I have flopped — fallen on my face.
Thus I am crawling to You once more
begging for forgiveness and renewal.

O God, why do I persist in reaching out for You
when I know full well that this won't be my last failure?
Why don't You set me free from this mortal shell
that is so permeated with sin and selfishness?
Why is it that with all my praying and pleading
and my sincere attempts to serve You
I still strike out when I come to bat?

Lord, I am like a blundering idiot.
I try to love — and I love unwisely.
I try to be selfless and generous —
and I'm suckered out of my savings.
I try to touch others with concern —
and my knuckles get rapped with scorn.
I try to communicate Your grace and judgments —
and it is thrown right back into my teeth.

I am tempted again and again,
and there are times when I cannot resist.
Am I responsible for this failure-fought nature of mine?
Am I to blame for its abominable soft spots?

Thus I come crawling to You again.
Keep my failings from threatening or hurting others about me.
Forgive me, O God, and forbid that a day should come
when I may be too discouraged and beaten down
to come crawling back to You.

The Church
Within the World

"You are the salt of the earth. . . . You are the light of the world."
(Matthew 5:13-14)

Pulpit-pounding is losing its appeal for the man on the street.
This may be the reason one seldom finds him in the pew.
The church may have to revert to the method which has always
    been effective, which is used with disturbing success by the
    enemies of our faith and our freedom,
    which in many areas of our world
    is the only possible method of witness that is left to us.
It is proclamation by means of infiltration.

How can I infiltrate my society as a son and servant
    of the living God?
By being the salt of the earth and the light of the world right
    where I am and wherever God's course may take me.

This does not mean I must preach on street corners
    or distribute tracts door to door.
It may not necessarily mean that I inaugurate or support
    movements for the abolishment of pornography
    or for censorship or liquor control.
I cannot condone the evils of society.
I must often condemn them.
But I may be far more effective by infiltrating
    my distraught world with the living proof
    that I have something far better
    and more meaningful and satisfying
    than so much of the crud that the multitudes
    are feeding on.
This is done by reaching the lonely, loveless, insecure, empty,
    meaningless souls all about me with the Gospel of God's love
    and acceptance.
It must be done by contemporary disciples of Christ,

by those who have experienced God's love and are learning how
to communicate this love to their fellowmen
through loving them.
It is done by being the salt of the earth
and the light of the world in their midst
and ultimately leading them to God's eternal love.

I am to be the salt of the earth.
But there are times when I do not appear to possess
that penetrating pungency which stays corruption
and manifests divine power.
Instead of my salting the earth,
the world often succeeds in corrupting me.
Like a broken toy, a dull knife, a burned-out fuse,
I become, in the words of my Lord, "good for nothing."

I am enjoined to be the salt of the earth
and the light of the world
right here where I am.
This is the real purpose of my existence
as a servant and priest of God.
I have heard the command of my Lord.

I have heard His promise of adequate grace and power
to enable me to carry out His command.
God forbid that my indifference to His command
and humanity's needs, and indifference that is promoted
by self-concern and self-indulgence,
may render me "good for nothing."

+   +   +

*Forgive me, O God, for proclaiming when I should have been infiltrating,
for failing so often to communicate Your power and provision into the
weakness and emptiness of my world. Restore me to discipleship, and grant
me the grace to truly be the salt of the earth and the light of the world.
Amen.*

Where
The Action Is

"As Thou didst send Me into the world, so I have sent them into the world." (John 17:18)

I am where the action is.
I live in the most exciting and challenging period
    of church history.
I am on the front lines of this the 20th century.

It is a period of great change.
Old things are passing away,
    and this includes some of the traditions,
    the ancient trappings and embellishments that are no longer
    relevant to this age.

The Christ to whom I am driven
    is not "a wooden Christ upon a wooden cross."
He is not a halo-crowned picture on the wall,
    a dead plaything that I invented,
    the figment of someone's imagination,
    a Linus blanket or sucking thumb that comforts and pacifies.
This is the Christ that many will worship.
This kind of Christ is not where the action is.
He most certainly is not relevant to the world in which I live.

I am a priest of the living Christ.
He is in the world about me.
He labors in the Peace Corps, the civil rights movement,
    the social welfare agencies, the courts of justice.
He is present in those churches that seek to communicate His love
    to the masses about them.
Wherever I turn, I can find Him at work,
    touching men with His healing,
    supporting men in their conflicts,
    saving men from their sins.

I don't have to look for Christ on some holy mountain
    or wait for Him in some hallowed sanctuary.
I need not search for Him at spiritual retreats
    or expect some revered saint to bring Him to me
    or travel to some far country in quest of the Holy Grail.

He is here!
And this is where the action is.

+ + +

*Forgive me, O Lord, for always running for my life, for looking for greener
pastures in which to serve. This is where You have placed me. This is
where You are. Enable me to recognize You here and to serve You here
as the living Christ. Amen.*

Reason
For Rejoicing

**"Do not rejoice in this, that the spirits are subject to you;
but rejoice that your names are written in heaven."** (Luke 10:20)

There is reason for rejoicing in that my significance before God
    is not dependent on the feeling or the fact of success.
My joy as a child of God is not to be measured
    by my accomplishments or achievements.
I am significant apart from success
    if I am rightly related to God through faith in Christ
    and if I walk in obedience to Him.
How do I know that my name is written in heaven?
I know that I am a forgiven and accepted son of God.
"Thou didst forgive the iniquity of Thy people;
    Thou didst pardon all their sin," proclaimed the psalmist.
"Thou hast cast all my sins behind Thy back," exclaimed Isaiah.
"I will forgive their iniquity,
    and I will remember their sin no more," I read in Jeremiah.

"There is therefore now no condemnation for those who are in Christ Jesus," wrote Paul.

I must bring my iniquities and wrongdoings to God.
I must recognize the glorious message and gift of salvation, that Jesus Christ has already suffered the consequences of guilt on my behalf.
I must entrust my life wholly and totally to the eternal promises of God.
I must accept these promises and the Christ of these promises.
Then I must rejoice in this relationship of faith in God.

"Beloved, we are God's children now," wrote John.
Truly, this is reason for rejoicing.

+   +   +

Eternal God, I rejoice in that I need not cite statistics or flaunt my achievements in order to establish my significance. I thank You for accepting me as I am, for adopting me into Your family, and for the promise to keep me forever. Amen.

Lest
I Be Disqualified

"I pommel my body and subdue it lest after preaching to others I myself should be disqualified." (1 Corinthians 9:27)

I am a son of God.
I have been reconciled to His kingdom, reunited to His family.
"But I keep going on," wrote Paul,
    "grasping ever more firmly
    that purpose for which Christ grasped me."

I am justified by faith.
But it is still necessary for me to keep the faith.
The failures in my life will be forgiven,
    but the failure to rise from defeat,
    to "keep going on" in my walk with God,
    may disqualify me for the final reward.
It means that I must give priority to this business
    of being Christian.
I must make whatever sacrifices are necessary to keep this first and
    foremost in my life.

"I do not run aimlessly," said Paul.
"I do not box as one beating the air."
There is a goal for my life.
This is what gives it meaning and purpose.
It is to travel within divine order and orbit.
It is to recognize my responsibility to God
    as His servant and disciple,
    to dedicate my life to His purposes in my community and world.
This is the reason for my existence.
I am here to communicate and demonstrate God's love to a broken
    and sin-ridden humanity.
If I fail to expend my God-given talents and gifts
    for this purpose, I stand in danger of being disqualified.

There is a reward for those who keep the faith.
It is not some sentimental, harp-playing, cloud-hopping,
    pearly-gate nonsense.
It is eternal reality, the answer to my deepest needs
    and longings.
It is the guaranteed result of faithful struggle
    in Christian conflict.

I don't need to be disqualified.
I live in an era of divine grace.
If I submit myself to God's love and to obedient servanthood,
    I will run the race successfully
    and am assured of the ultimate prize.

+ + +

O God, forbid that I should ever lay down my arms. Grant that I may by Your grace rise from every defeat to engage afresh the enemy of my soul, to run the race before me, to fulfill Your purposes in my world about me. Amen.

The Fraternity Of the Fearful

"When he saw the wind, he was afraid, and beginning to sink he cried out, 'Lord, save me.' " (Matthew 14:30)

Why am I so tense today?
I feel adrift in a strange sea with crosscurrents pulling
    this way and that,
        without star or compass to guide me.

Anxiety is the result of not knowing who we are
    and to whom we belong.
But I know who I am.
I know to whom I belong.
I even know where I am going.
Yet I am anxious and afraid.

It must be because I am looking at the wind
    rather than the Lord of the wind.
I am tossed by the tumult about me and torn by the contradictions
    within me.

I cannot ignore the storm that rages
    or escape the conflict in which I am involved
    or turn away from the burdens that tax my strength.
But I can focus anew on that One
    who is in the midst of the storm,

who will stand with me through the conflict,
who will not bend under this life's heavy burdens.

I need to recognize again my identity.
"We have received adoption as sons," writes Paul.
"And if a son then an heir."
I must reestablish my confidence in His continual presence.
"Even though I walk through the valley of the shadow of death,"
    proclaims the psalmist,
    "I fear no evil, for Thou art with me."
I must reaffirm my faith in His promises.
"You will be sorrowful, but your sorrow will turn into joy,"
    said Jesus.
"This is the victory that overcomes the world, our faith,"
    proclaimed the apostle John.

I may not always have peace of mind.
But I need not belong to the fraternity of the fearful.

+   +   +

*Great God, I look for You amidst the conflicts and contradictions of this
life, but I do not see You. It is because I look through the eyes of this frail
body rather than the eyes of faith. Help me to see You through faith today
and to stand firm and confident in the midst of the storm that rages about
me. Amen.*

Epiphany
Through Me

**"Having gifts that differ according to the grace given to us,
let us use them." (Romans 12:6)**

I am appointed to be the epiphany of Christ
    in my distraught world.

Before this is possible,
  I must acknowledge that I am a person of worth.
This significance is not something I acquire or merit through
  personal effort.
It began with creation, when man was made
  in the spiritual image of God.
It was abused and distorted when that image was fractured.
It was restored in the redemption of Jesus Christ,
  when man was set free from sin's guilt
  and ushered into the saving grace of God.

This recognition of my personal worth
  is enhanced by the revelation
  that I possess divine gifts.
It is in the effective use of these gifts that I give expression
  to the feeling and the fact of my significance.
It is in the unselfish use of these gifts that I declare
  and demonstrate the epiphany of Jesus Christ.

Before I can demonstrate the epiphany in terms of activity,
  I must rightfully manifest it in terms of attitudes.
"Let love be genuine," exhorted the apostle.
Apart from faith in God and love of fellowman
  my gifts will serve no one.
Genuine love is truly a reflection of the epiphany.
It is the center and core of effective service.
It is that eternal quality which will turn my modest gifts
  into powerful tools that build God's kingdom
  and accomplish His purposes.

My personal worth is not measured by the plaudits of men.
My gifts may not be noticed by others.
My participation in and reflection of Christ's epiphany is not
  scored by statistics or human success figures.
When God has His way in and through me,
  the epiphany of Jesus Christ will be manifested in a dark
  and demon-infested world.

+ + +

I thank You, O God, for the gifts You have entrusted to me. I need Your help that I may use them correctly in order to demonstrate something of Christ's epiphany in the world about me. Amen.

When Life
Has Meaning

"I chose you and appointed you that you should go and bear fruit." (John 15:16)

If I am to discover health and happiness even in the midst of
life's conflicts and distortions,
   my life must be permeated with purpose and meaning.
"He who has a WHY to live can bear almost any HOW,"
   said an old philosopher.
"Do not labor for the food which perishes but for the food which
   endures to eternal life," said Jesus.

There must first be housecleaning and cleansing.
I must be delivered from those selfish goals that have blinded
   my eyes to truth and reality.
I must be rid of the husks that have stifled my soul.
I must recognize that I can no longer live for myself.
   that such will always lead me up blind alleys and
   down dead-end streets.

Then I must reach out for new meaning and purpose.
"I am the Bread of Life," said Jesus.
   "He who comes to Me shall not hunger, and he who believes
   in Me shall never thirst."
It is in the love and grace of God that empty souls find filling,
   guilty hearts find forgiving, purposeless lives find
   objective and design.

This must be followed by commitment.
I must commit myself subjectively to the Person of Christ.
I must also commit myself objectively and practically to the
   purposes of Christ.
I cannot truly experience Christ in faith unless I follow
   Him in servanthood.

This commitment must be total and perpetual.
This becomes my purpose in life;
   it gives eternal meaning to my life.
My job, my interpersonal relationships, my tangible pleasures
   may remain much the same.
But in them and through them I am the priest and servant of God.

My friends may forsake me,
   earth's tragedies reduce me to poverty,
   but Christ and His purpose for my life will never let me go.

+   +   +

*Eternal God, forgive me for cluttering up my life with self-centered
ambitions. Restore me to Your orbit and design for me. May this sense of
divine purpose and goal keep me steady amid the convulsions and conster-
nations of this life. Amen.*

How to
Start Over Again

"You must be born anew." (John 3:7)

It is one of life's most precious gifts:
   the opportunity and the privilege to begin anew,
   to start over again.

Even my original entry into this world was stained with sin.
I inherited an error-prone nature.

I was born into a discordant, disease-ridden humanity.
I manifested a fractured personality.
I was destined to be a failure.

But inculcated into my soul was the longing for better things,
    the grasp for perfection,
    the urge for something
    that hovered tantalizingly beyond my reach.

I flail the air with desire but fail to obtain.
I run but never arrive.
I seek but do not find.
I grovel and grapple with the things of this life only to lapse
    into depression and defeat, my soul empty and unfulfilled.

My great God has shown me how to start over again.
It begins with a new birth,
    a reentry into this dimension of finite experience
    with the realization of divine acceptance and grace.
It is the gift of the ever-loving Creator.
It is revealed through the redemption of His Son.
It is applicable to those who have failed.
It is received and appropriated by faith.

I am still haunted by failure and plagued with defeat.
The new birth does not promise the end to guilt feelings
    or to the sins and weaknesses that cause them.
But even while clothed
    in the blemishes
    and flaws of mortal flesh,
    I am the adopted son of God.
My failures do not damn or destroy me.
They drive me back to the sufficiency of God.
There I find forgiveness and acceptance.
There I am granted the opportunity to start over again.

+   +   +

I claim, O God, Your forgiveness for the failings and faults of my earth-bound nature. I seek, O God, the grace and the courage to begin again. May I remember always Your victory over sin and death. May I see some reflection of that victory in my daily circumstances. Amen.

Why Some People Can't Love

"He who is forgiven little loves little." (Luke 7:47)

I find it difficult to love certain people.
I can easily respond to those who love me.
I am eager to return affection and adoration to those who
    meet my needs.
I cannot find within me the grace to love those who do not
    gratefully receive my love, who do not love me in return.

The need of our world is for that love which gushes forth
    like a spring to give value and worth
    to the person one loves.
It must be the kind of love that is not dependent on
    affable or affectionate response.

This kind of love has its origin in God alone.
I can portray it only insofar as I receive of and abide
    in God's love.
I must daily face up to my need for His mercy.
How utterly I have failed and grieved Him!
How great is that love which is capable of accepting me
    despite my sins,
        of taking upon Himself the consequences of my wrongdoings,
        of reconciling and reinstating me in His life and purposes!
It is when I understand something of divine forgiveness
    that I make way for love in my soul.
It is in the measure that I accept God's eternal love
    that I discover the capability to love others.

When I am incapable of loving others
I am dabbling with damnation.
It portrays that I am not fully aware
of my own faults and failings,
my atrocities before God and man.
When I confess my iniquities, it is with a glib tongue.
I am simply not cognizant of the immensity of my sin,
of how much I need God's forgiveness.
But when I see myself as I am
and recognize that God is willing to accept me as I am,
then I should not find it difficult to love others.

If some people can't love,
it is because they have not realized the experience
or comprehended the meaning of God's redeeming love.
When I find myself incapable of loving,
it ought to return me to the mourner's bench
to contemplate anew my ugly sins
and to seek afresh God's loving forgiveness.

+ + +

Loving God, You have borne my sin and accepted me as Your son. Your love is far too much for me to comprehend, but may I understand enough about it to receive from its saving and transforming power the capability of loving those who are difficult to love. Amen.

Divine Words
For a Dark World

"Sell your possessions and give alms; provide yourselves with purses that do not grow old." (Luke 12:33)

I have God's recipe for happy, meaningful living
in a discordant world.

It is also the key to contributive living
   in respect to the inmates of this world.
I am first enjoined to "sell."
It means that I am to give up anything and deny myself everything
   that stands in the way of God's will for my life.
I must take my selfish fingers off that which I classify as mine:
   my possessions, my talents, my very life.
In order to inherit heaven, I must willingly disinherit earth
   and its lesser values.
Christ must come first in my life, or He does not come at all.

He exhorts me to "give."
What good I have received is from God.
This does not make it my sole possession.
It is mine to enjoy; it is also mine to give.
It is destined to meet the needs of men about me.
When I neglect to give, I become a dead-end street,
   a stagnant pool.
Where there is no outlet, there will cease to be inflow.
My life is supposed to be a warm, loving, sunlit room
   where others may enter and help themselves to what they need.
"Inasmuch as you do it for one of these, My little ones,
   you do it for Me," said my Lord.

He advises me to "invest."
I am to spend my earthbound years laying up the kind of wealth
   that will stand up to His stern and unerring judgment.
My stocks and bonds and savings accounts will not pass this kind
   of inspection.
I am to invest my life and possessions
   in terms of the hungry that need feeding,
   the naked that need clothing,
   the sick and needy that need visiting and comforting,
   the souls that need saving.
These are the investments that pay off in this life
   and the next.

I am living on borrowed time.
If I am to discover purpose and meaning for my life,
   I had better live it according to the divine prescription.

+ + +

*O God, I have been the recipient of many good gifts. I have hoarded them
for my selfish enjoyment. Teach me how to use them and to invest them in
the welfare of others and thereby to discover their true meaning and value
for my life. Amen.*

Christians
On Trial

**"Everyone who acknowledges Me before men I also will
acknowledge before My Father who is in heaven." (Matthew
10:32)**

Christians today are being forced to rediscover and redefine
  the church.
I am in the process of rediscovering and redefining
  the Christian.

The church can no longer be defined by denominational handles
  or confined to buildings and institutions
  or scored by impressive budgets, affluent congregations,
  or massive membership rolls.
The church will continue to exist within these structures
  and be included in these statistics.
It is equally prominent and often more significant in the groups
  of Christians who meet in homes and offices, on residential
  streets, or in industrial complexes.

As a Christian today, I am also on trial.
I have been satisfied with membership in the local congregation
  and participation in the sacraments.
I have performed all the exercises and said all the right words.
I have accepted Jesus as my Lord and Savior.
But this has not produced in me the kind of fervor and power

that motivated the members of the first-century church.
I have not made the impact on my community
that they did on theirs.
When I compare my faith with theirs
I provoke some very frustrating feelings
about the authenticity of my faith.

Then I contemplate Christ's call to discipleship.
He called on His disciples to love one another,
to take up the cross, to renounce all that they had,
to endure hardship and sacrifice,
to lose their lives for His sake.
He pointed to the dearest and holiest of human affections,
their families and loved ones,
and claimed for Himself a prior devotion.
He insisted that for His sake
and for the benefit of humanity about them
they must be prepared to accept the worst suffering
and the uttermost ignominy.

I got away with apathetic professions up to now.
I was able to hide my lethargy or halfheartedness
under soft symbols and loud exclamations.
I have never really suffered for Christ.
I haven't lived up to the prerequisites of my Master.
I have not loved my fellowman as myself.
I have looked the other way when my brother was oppressed.
I eat three meals a day while he may get only one.
I invest for retirement while he has no promise of a tomorrow.
Inasmuch as I have failed to extend myself
in self-sacrificing love to my brothers,
I have failed to love God and to serve Christ, whose disciple
I claim to be.

Today I am on trial.
I must put up or shut up.

+ + +

O God, give me the courage to face up to the demands of discipleship, and the grace to meet them. May I begin today, even in some small way, to relate as Your son and servant to someone whose path I will cross and whose life I may influence. Amen.

The Call
Of Christ

"As Jesus passed on from there, He saw a man called Matthew sitting at the tax office; and He said to him, 'Follow Me.' "
(Matthew 9:9)

The most astounding, incredible fact of all history is the
   call of Christ to sinful man,
   the invitation to follow Him.
It is extended to the meanest, cruelest,
   most unpromising creatures on the face of the earth.
No matter how fractured or distorted,
   failure-fraught or inadequate I may be,
   I am invited to follow Jesus Christ, to become a son of God,
   a servant and disciple of my Lord and Savior.

It is not an invitation to casual acquaintance or weekly worship.
It is not an offer of outside help when I am on the spot.
It is the call to follow Him.

I have bowed before a multiplicity of gods.
I have attempted to confine Christ to some Sunday-morning corner
   of my life.
I have often used Him when I ran up against some incalculable,
   unsolvable problem in my life.
I really know little of what it means to follow Him.

The call to follow Christ is the invitation to become
  exclusively attached to the Person of Christ.
It is not an abstract theology or a flock of ideals.

It is Jesus Christ, God incarnate,
  and I am invited to love Him, serve Him, and crown Him Lord
  of every phase and facet, attitude and aspect of my life.
To follow Christ must mean dedication to the purposes as well as
  to the Person of Christ,
  to loving, serving, sacrificing, and dying for the humanity
  that Christ came to serve and to save.
It is possible to daily confess one's sins and still remain
  indifferent to and detached from the purposes of Christ.

Of course I accept Jesus Christ.
This ought to flood my life with the joy of sin forgiven and
  the assurance of life eternal.
But if I am to be effective as a Christian and obedient as a
  son of God, I must follow Jesus Christ.

I do not know where He will lead me.
I do know that such a course will involve me in demonstrating
  my love for Him in and through the lives
  of my fellowmen about me.

+   +   +

*I thank You, O God, for the invitation to follow You. I thank You because
You accept me as I am. Now, great God, make me what I ought to be.
Yesterday I followed my selfish inclinations. Today enable me to truly
follow You regardless of what it may cost. Amen.*

If I
Really Believed

"He is not here; for He has risen." (Matthew 28:6)

I say I believe in the risen Christ.
I confess my faith in the living Lord every time I attend
    my church or pray in His name.
What ought to happen in my life
    if I really believed that Jesus was raised from the dead?

If I really believed,
    I would fling aside my garments of self-righteousness,
    cast off the window dressing of my life,
    and fall on my face in repentance of sin.

If I really believed in the living Christ,
    He would be the most important factor in my life.
He would take first place among all loyalties and allegiances.

If I really believed that Jesus lives,
    my life would be filled with joy unspeakable,
    peace incomprehensible.   ,
I would not be anxious about the morrow
    or afflicted with guilt feelings out of the past.
And the joy that Jesus gives would be more satisfying
    than all the foolish thrills of the world.

If I really believed in the resurrected Christ,
    no problem or difficulty, weakness or sin,
    insufficiency or inadequacy could destroy me.
I would discover that the power which took Christ from the grave
    cannot be baffled by my thwarting frailties,
    that the God who performed
    this splendid feat of might and glory
    could certainly handle my little pains and problems.

If I really believed in the risen Christ,
    I would be eager to bypass life's comforts and conveniences,
    even a few of its legitimate needs,
    in order that the resurrection message might reach all men
    throughout the world.
I would take up the cross assigned to me and endure suffering and
    sacrifice in the endeavor to communicate God's love to sick
    and lonely souls about me.

If I really believed that Christ arose from the grave,
    I would cease fretting about the godlessness of my world,
    the tumult and turmoil about me.
I would cease worrying about my status and welfare and dedicate
    my energies to the task of proclaiming that Christ has risen
    and is my living Lord.
If I really believed.

+   +   +

*O Lord, help me to believe that You were truly raised from the dead, and
help me to demonstrate Your resurrection power in my life and living. Amen.*

My Place
In the Sun

"He who believes in Me will also do the works that I do."
(John 14:12)

I have found my place in the sun.
I am to carry on the purposes of the incarnate Christ.
I have been redeemed and empowered to interpret and
    communicate the healing and saving love of God
    to a distraught world.

I must do this creatively.
Here I am engaged as a co-worker with God.
I have been a part of the chaos of this rebellious world.
Now I am dedicated to bringing God's order
    back into this world's chaos.
Where there is hatred I must sow love.
Where there are wounds I must give healing.
Where there is despair I must proclaim hope.
Where there is darkness I must shed light.
I must share in the creation of institutions of mercy,
    hospitals to heal our sick,
        schools to educate our young,
            Christian homes to bless our communities.

Christ redeemed me through His sacrificial love.
I act to express His love toward others.
I need not expend my energies for my salvation.
But I must dedicate them to the salvation of others.
I am to bring Christ to my neighbor and my neighbor to Christ.
This must be done by proclamation.
It must also be done by demonstration.
I must learn how to portray to my fellowman a loving, redeeming,
    accepting, forgiving God.
I can do this only if I reflect these divine qualities in
    my person and personality.
I cannot do this by myself.
I must work in harmony with other members of Christ's body.
I must allow God's Spirit to use me
    as a member of that fellowship.

I have found my place in the sun.
It is here — right where I am.
It includes joys and sorrows, successes and defeats,
    bright moments and dark hours.
It demands obedience and loyalty to my Creator and Redeemer.
It relies on the empowering and motivating
    of His ever-present Spirit.
It promises the satisfaction and enrichment of purposeful living.
This is my place in the sun.

+ + +

You have, O God, not only redeemed me, but You have chosen me and empowered me through Your Spirit to proclaim Your work of redemption. Help me not only to realize my identity as Your son but my responsibility as Your servant. Amen.